Mayberry Momma's™
Food for the
Soul and Body

Jewell Mitchell Kutzer

Dynamic Living Press
St. Augustine, Florida

Mayberry Momma's™ *Food for the Soul and Body*

Copyright © 2006 by Jewell Mitchell Kutzer. All rights reserved. No part of this book may be used, reproduced or transmitted in any form or by any means, electronic or mechanical, including photocopying or recording, or by any information storage and retrieval system, without written permission, except in the case of brief quotations embodied in articles or reviews. For information, contact the publisher: Dynamic Living Press, P.O. Box 3164, St. Augustine, FL 32085-3164.

Excerpts from *Memories of Mayberry: A Nostalgic Look at Andy Griffith's Hometown, Mount Airy, North Carolina* by Jewell Mitchell Kutzer, copyright © 2001 by Jewell Mitchell Kutzer. Reprinted by permission of Dynamic Living Press

Front cover flap photo of Momma courtesy of Louis Hocevar Videography

Inclusion of the "Famous Pork Chop Sandwich" with the permission of Charles and Mary Dowell, owners of the Snappy Lunch in Mount Airy, North Carolina

Disclaimer: This book is not connected with *The Andy Griffith Show*, nor has it been created, licensed, authorized or endorsed by Mayberry Enterprises, Danny Thomas Enterprises, Andy Griffith, Viacom, Inc., or CBS, Inc. and their successors in interest.

Cover and interior design and formatting by Bookwrights.com

Printed in the United States of America

Cataloging-in-Publication Data

Kutzer, Jewell Mitchell.
Mayberry Momma's™ Food for the Soul and Body / Jewell Mitchell Kutzer–1st. ed.
    p. cm.
  ISBN-13: 978-0-971100-05-3
  ISBN-10: 0-971100-05-5
  1. Cookery - American–Southern style 2. Food habits–Southern States
  3. Spiritual life–Anecdotes 4. Mount Airy, N.C. I. Title
TX715.K88 2007
641.5975–dc22

2006907663

Contents

SECTION ONE: *From Biscuits to Yeast Rolls*

SECTION TWO: *Some Food for the Soul*

SECTION THREE: *From the Garden*

Thank You!

I guarantee you, honey, a lot of encouragement and support, both technical and loving, was necessary to put this book together.

First, I must give credit to my fantastic publicist, **Leigh Cort**. Sublimely sophisticated, but with her heart in the right place and her feet on the ground, she encouraged (or perhaps pushed) me to get into print all my many musings about food and family in the South. A longtime member of the International Food, Wine & Travel Writers, Leigh helped coordinate the nationwide recipe contest, making sure the word got out.

Second, I gratefully acknowledge the immensely important contribution of **Chef David S. Bearl**, Director and Coordinator of the Southeastern Culinary Institute. David took time out from his detailed duties in far-flung areas to oversee the judging of the recipes received in the contest. Every entry got personal treatment and specific responses. For instance, one recipe called for 2 cups of "good chicken broth." David wrote on the sheet "As opposed to bad chicken broth?" This man is not only an acknowledged culinary expert, but also a warm, loving genius!

Then there are my fellow members of the ASAP group in St. Augustine, Florida: **Frances Keiser, Jeannine Auth, and Karen Harvey.** All are authors with books in the marketplace that aim to make a difference! Support, new ideas and constructive criticism were dealt out in equal measure as my new book took life.

And a big hug to that wonderful woman, **Ann Vaughn**, who helped coordinate things in my hometown of Mount Airy, North Carolina. Ann's as sweet as she is smart!

And, as always, my daughter, **Ellen I. Davis**. She was on the scene in spades when my first book was published and, although now living on the other side of the state, was there for me again. Ellen was especially helpful in editing the "Food for the Soul" chapters. She understands and supports my desire to communicate uplifting thoughts.

And to you, the readers, who cared enough to take this book into your hearts and homes.

Hello From The Mayberry Momma™

I grew up in the same small town as Andy Griffith, one of America's most beloved entertainers. Our hometown, Mount Airy, North Carolina, provided much inspiration for the atmosphere of television's *Mayberry*. Our town's residents were reflected in the down-to-earth and quirky folks we all loved on *The Andy Griffith Show* and *Mayberry, R.F.D.* In fact, when Andy and I were growing up there my grandfather was the Justice of the Peace and I, like TV's *Opie*, played around in the jail.

The *Mayberry Momma™* is my alter ego—an upbeat, feisty Southern lady of mature years. A blend of TV's *Aunt Bee* and my real Aunt Bea, Momma is saucy, funny and lovingly in-your-face. As a Motivational Humorist, I perform as the Mayberry Momma for conferences and conventions all over the country.

As a good Southern girl (I'll use that term 'til I die, thank you) the delights of food are never far from my mind. That's why I launched a nation wide search for the best "down-home" recipes to include in this book. I also asked the cooks to include a personal story that was connected to the recipe so we would know why that particular dish was a favorite.

You'll find the Grand Prize winning recipe, "Cindy's Git Along Home Chicken Casserole," as well as the winners in all the other categories inside. In addition, a number of other contest entries were just too good to leave out. So get your tasting spoon ready!

In this book I share some special memories, some "soul food" I grew up with, and some words of homespun wisdom. Since "Man does not live by bread alone," I hope you will also find some nourishment for the soul in these pages.

Thanks for spending time with me and I hope you enjoy these "lickin' good eatin'" dishes.

In the Mayberry Spirit!

Jewell Mitchell Kutzer
aka the Mayberry Momma™

Author of: Memories of Mayberry: A Nostalgic Look at Andy Griffith's Hometown: Mount Airy, North Carolina. ISBN: 0-9711000-4.
http://www.memoriesofmayberry.com

Preface

ood and philosophy were dished out in equal portions at the dinner table of my youth. Whenever I helped with the cooking process, Grandmother would not only instruct in the details of how the ingredients in the recipe fit together, but also took time to draw out of me any concerns that had come up in school that day, suggesting approaches that would most likely produce a better ending to the story.

When I think of the variety of food that Grandmother put on the table, and with such seeming ease, I am amazed. None of today's supposed time and energy saving appliances or gadgets were available to her in the 40's. A large wooden spoon was the utensil most used for "beating, folding, mixing," and a number of other cooking instructions. The metal hand-cranked eggbeater seemed to be saved for making "special" dishes. No rolls of aluminum foil existed, just trusty wax paper.

I really laughed when I recently saw a commercial touting a new and improved covering for a bowl of leftovers. It consisted of opaque plastic sewn to an elastic band. We thought that was dandy in the late '40's also. It was all we had. No Tupperware was available for our cupboards. An oilcloth tablecloth covered the metal kitchen table and, while we had graduated to an electric stove when I began to help with the cooking, I clearly remember the wood-burning stove of earlier years.

We made do with what we had. Many's the time I was given an empty cardboard Quaker Oats container with the instructions to cover it with a scrap of fabric (perhaps the remnant of a flour sack) so that it could be used for a new purpose. Recycle—you bet! Over and over again. "Waste not-want not" was the constant motto.

During the school day I was taught readin', writin', and 'rithmetic. In the evenings my grandfather taught me caring and correct behavior. During the years he served as Justice of the Peace and U.S. Marshal he had seen a lot of people "go wrong," and as he spun his tales, he gently weaved in the instruction I needed to "do the right thing."

Certainly hope you enjoy these servings of nourishment for both the soul and body. Sometimes it may be a particular dish that seems to be "soul satisfying." Then again, it may be the turn of a phrase that fills you up.

Eat Hearty!

SECTION ONE

From Biscuits to Yeast Rolls

Rising in Love

My nose registered the first alert, picking up the unmistakable smell of yeast rising from hot, still-baking dinner rolls. Dropping my third-grade school books in the parlor, I headed straight for the kitchen, only to find Lillian, our cook, just about to put the last batch in the oven. A big sigh announced my disappointment. I had missed my part. It was my job to beat the dough down after it had risen up almost over the edge of the brown and blue striped crockery mixing bowl. The bowl might as well have been fine china from the care taken with it, in spite of a couple of thumb-sized chips on the rim. Perhaps it was the fact that it housed the beginning of a miracle: light, flavorful rolls, without which the evening meal would have been incomplete. The love that infused the baking process gave this particular bowl semi-divine properties.

Lillian spoke to me in her deep, sweet voice, "Chile, you're late. Had to get the rolls movin'—couldn't wait on ya." I apologized with a hug, pressing my pigtailed head deep into her ample dark bosom.

"I'm sorry, I was jumping rope with Sylvia and plumb forgot the time." I explained, receiving a generous dusting of flour from the printed apron hanging around her neck. It was a brand new apron, even though the last one had only been worn for a couple of months. Grandmother had bought the apron, one of many fine-looking specimens. She would have preferred to buy Lillian new dresses, but that just wasn't done, and even if she had, Lillian would have been too proud to accept them. So Grandmother did her part to enhance Lillian's meager wardrobe with bright, wonderfully decorated aprons.

However, once used a short time, Grandmother would decide that each apron was no longer suitable, and replace it, giving the old ones to Lillian for "rags." If Lillian's grandchildren were ever seen wearing dresses made of similar material, no mention was ever made of it. Both Grandmother and Lillian would keep their dignity.

Since Grandmother valued industriousness, I was glad to be found wiping off the counters and putting things away when she came through the green swinging door that led to the kitchen from the hall.

"How's it comin' along, Lillian?" she inquired, glancing around the room.

"Right fine, Mizz Ellen," Lillian replied. (This more familiar name was employed with family, but it would have been "Mizz Creed" had any outsiders been present.)

"Jewell," Grandmother continued, "make sure you pay 'tention to what Lillian shows you. You'll have to know how to do this when you cook for a family of yer own some day."

I often thought it curious that my mother, her daughter, showed no interest in making anything more involved than simple desserts. Surely Grandmother had tried to produce in my mother this same sense of responsibility for delicious meals for the family. Nevertheless, I was proud that Grandmother thought me worthy of instruction, and silently promised not to let her down.

"Let me look at your school work in the parlor when you're through, Jewell," Grandmother said, as she refastened a large tortoise shell hairpin into the soft bun of dark hair on the back of her head. Satisfied that meal preparations were proceeding well, she turned with a smile and walked back into the hall.

I spied the special mixing bowl, a small amount of dough still clinging to its inside. With my fingers I swiftly lifted the dough out and into my mouth. Raw dough, what a delight! I loved it so! I could taste the developing flavor of those exquisite rolls that would be served later. Even as I ran my fingers around the bowl, I did so with reverence.

Usually I would eat a lot of dough, as much as would have made two or three rolls for baking. Lillian would caution me against eating too much, so as not to spoil my supper. But for me, eating dough nourished my spirit as much as my body.

Later, at suppertime, when the browned and glazed rolls appeared in the linen-covered bowl on the table, it seemed a marvel to my seven-year old mind. With each delicious, butter-soaked bite, I tasted the essence of the yeast, of Lillian, and of love.

Even my beloved grandfather admitted to me one evening after dinner, "When I pray, 'Give us this day our daily bread'—frankly, I'm thinkin' of Lillian's yeast rolls."

 Check out "Best Buns Ever"

Square Deal Sour Cream Rye Biscuits

Lillian Julow
Gainesville, Florida

Ingredients:

3 cups all-purpose flour
1 cup rye flour
2 ½ teaspoons baking powder
1 tablespoon caraway seeds
4 tablespoons (1/4 cup) cold unsalted butter, sliced

1 large egg
½ cup whole sour cream
1 ¼ cups whole milk
½ teaspoon salt

Preparation:

Preheat oven to 400 degrees.

In a food processor combine the all-purpose flour and rye flour, baking powder, caraway seeds, and salt. Add cold butter, close lid, and pulse/chop until mixture resembles coarse crumbs.

With a fork, in a small bowl, beat egg, sour cream and milk together. Add to flour mixture and pulse just until dry ingredients are moistened.

Turn out onto a floured surface and gently knead 6 or 8 times. Transfer dough to a greased baking sheet and pat into a ½-inch-thick square or rectangle. Cut into 3-inch squares, but do not separate.

Bake 17 to 22 minutes or until golden brown. Serve hot or warm, split open and slathered with butter.

For a real Southern delicacy, stuff the hot biscuits with ham. Those yummy Ham Biscuits will disappear in a hurry.

7

Behind the Recipe

Square Deal Sour Cream Rye Biscuits

These "Square Deal" biscuits came out of my childhood in Lancaster, Pennsylvania - Amish country, though we were not Amish.

My mom called them "Square Deal" for two reasons. First, she couldn't see the sense in making biscuits round and wasting all that good dough in-between the circles. Plus, re-rolling the scraps only resulted in tough biscuits. Her solution? Make 'em square. We loved them, no matter what the shape.

Second reason - it was the mid-30s and the middle of the Depression. President Franklin Delano Roosevelt's New Deal was in full swing and lots of folks who couldn't find jobs were finally put to work when the WPA (Works Projects Administration) opened opportunities for them.

We were lucky because my father was a master butcher and worked for the same market chain for many years. And that's why FDR's New Deal became my mother's Square Deal.

Lillian Julow

Best Buns Ever

Kelly Jo Surbeck
Lusk, Wyoming

Ingredients

2 cups warm water (not hot)

2 packages of yeast (4 1/2 tsp.)

½ cup of granulated sugar

2 teaspoons salt

¼ cup of vegetable oil

1 egg, beaten, not whipped

6½ to 7 cups of all-purpose or bread flour

Preparation:

Combine all but the flour in large bowl. Add 3 to 4 cups of flour and mix well with a mixer. Knead in as much of the remaining flour as dough picks up.

Cover and let rise in a warm place. Immediately shape into buns or rolls.

Let rise and bake in preheated 400-degree oven for 13-15 minutes. While still warm, butter the slightly brown tops of buns. Butter will sink in and add additional flavor to the scrumptious mix!

Best homemade buns I've ever had.

I'm not sure where my momma got this recipe, but it's one of my most fond memories—smelling the bread rise, then bake.

I've always been a bread lover, but this takes the cake. Momma varies the size of the buns. Often times she will make them big enough that the ones left over from dinner can be frozen and used again later as sandwich buns or handy snacks.

Mashed Potato Yeast Scones

Susan Bazan
Sequim, Washington

Ingredients:

Scones

½ cup mashed potatoes (not instant)

½ cup shortening, melted (Crisco)

2 cups scalded milk

⅓ cup granulated sugar

1 pkg. dry yeast

½ cup lukewarm water

6 cups all-purpose flour

1 teaspoon baking powder

1 teaspoon salt

½ teaspoon baking soda

Vegetable oil for frying - enough to have a depth of 3" in pan. (4-6 cups depending on size of pan.) Note: Since these cook so quickly an 8 or 10 inch pan works fine.

Glaze/Topping

3 cups powdered sugar

1 tablespoon cocoa

1 teaspoon vanilla extract

1 teaspoon maple extract

1 tablespoon cinnamon

⅓ cup granulated sugar

Warm water

Preparation:

Mix potatoes, shortening, milk and ⅓ cup sugar together in large bowl. Cool to lukewarm. Add yeast dissolved in warm water. Add flour, baking powder, salt, and baking soda and mix well. Knead thoroughly. Dough will be slightly sticky. Grease top of dough, cover and refrigerate overnight. Dough will rise.

Next day, remove dough from refrigerator. Punch down dough. Roll out dough to 1/4 inch thickness on lightly floured surface. Cut in strips 1½ inches x 4 inches. Fry immediately in deep hot oil, turning once until brown on both sides (2 minutes.) Remove from oil and drain on paper towels. While still warm, dip top of scone in choice of glaze. Let glazed or sugared scones rest on waxed paper a few minutes after topping them. Eat and enjoy!

For Glaze/Topping:

Place ingredients in small bowls and stir until mixed.

Chocolate:
 1 cup powdered sugar, 1 tablespoon cocoa, and 1 tablespoon water

Vanilla:
 1 cup powdered sugar, 1 teaspoon vanilla extract, and 1 tablespoon water

Maple:
 1 cup powdered sugar, 1 teaspoon maple extract, and 1 tablespoon water

Cinnamon Sugar:
 ⅓ cup granulated sugar and 1 tablespoon of cinnamon.

Makes 36 scones

We always had these scones at Christmas as far back as I can remember. We went to Grandma and Grandpa's house. Christmas morning began with grandma frying these and having hot chocolate for the children and coffee for the adults. The fun part was getting to choose what glaze you wanted and getting to eat as many as you wanted!

Years later, as an adult, I realized that we were "poor" financially. Even though the presents under the tree were not plentiful, the good feelings we shared were in abundance. The Christmas scones were as important as the presents under the tree.

Miss Georgia's Buttermilk Cheese Biscuits

Jimmie Ann Abner
St. Simons Island, Georgia

Ingredients:

2 cups of White Lily self-rising flour
¼ cup of Crisco shortening
¾ cup of buttermilk
2 cups of coarsely grated sharp cheddar cheese

Preparation:

Preheat oven to 500 degrees

Measure flour into bowl by spooning into the measuring cup and leveling off with the back of the knife.

Cut in shortening until mixture resembles coarse crumbs. Add the grated cheese to this mixture. Blend in just enough buttermilk with fork until dough leaves sides of bowl. (Too much buttermilk makes dough too sticky to handle; not enough buttermilk makes dough dry. Also, for tender biscuits, always handle dough gently.)

Drop by tablespoonfuls onto greased baking sheet. (One inch apart for crusty biscuits; almost touching for soft sides.) Bake for 8 to 10 minutes. Serve at once.

Makes 12 two-inch biscuits.

This was my mother's recipe. Miss Georgia, as she was known to all, was a loving southern woman from Jesup, Georgia. Cooking was her love and her cheese biscuits were known far and wide by many people. In fact, the son of one of her friends had a serious brain operation, and when he came out of the anesthesia, he was asked what he felt like he could eat. His immediate answer was, "I want some of Miss Georgia's cheese biscuits."

She always used her hands to make the dough into round balls and flatten them out lightly onto a baking sheet with the back side of three fingers (index, middle, and ring.) This is an acquired art. If you want to try it, be sure to keep plenty of flour on your hands and sprinkle the wet dough with flour. It's easier to just spoon the dough onto the cookie sheet, but Miss Georgia wouldn't hear of doing it that way.

Her recipe is an adaptation of the White Lily biscuit recipe. She always used only White Lily Self-Rising Flour, because she knew nothing else would give you the same lightness and texture.

Back when electric stoves came into being, the electric companies in the South teamed up with food manufacturers and put on cooking shows. Those shows, of course, featured the sponsor's products. Those early interactions with local women produced a lot of brand loyalty which has been passed down through the generations. So I wasn't surprised to see quite a few recipes come in featuring a particular brand. My own grandmother was fiercely loyal to certain brands and I find myself still today favoring those for my cooking.

Broccoli Corn Bread

Joy Coats
McKinney, Texas

Ingredients:

2 boxes Jiffy corn bread mix
4 eggs
⅓ cup milk
1 stick margarine - soft
1 10 oz. box chopped frozen broccoli (thawed)
1 small onion, chopped
8 oz. sharp cheddar cheese - grated

Preparation:

Preheat oven to 375 degrees.

Place cornbread mix in large bowl. Add margarine, eggs, and milk. Beat well. Fold in broccoli, onion and cheese.

Spray 9 x 13 pan. Pour mixture in pan and bake at 375 degrees for 30-35 minutes until golden brown. Cut in squares.

I guarantee you that Mrs. Coats has made many a serving of cornbread the "old fashioned" way. Now she feels that simple suits her fine. Following is more about this fine lady.

Good Old Days?

JOY COATS, whose recipe for Broccoli Corn Bread precedes, is a delightful 79 years young Texas lady who says she learned to ski at the age of 55. Here are her thoughts on cooking and eating in the "good old days."

I remember growing up on a farm during the depression near Greenville, Texas. Margarine was bought by the pound. White in color, with a packet of yellow powder that had to be mixed by hand so it would look like butter. What a job!

After the cows quit giving milk, all our milk was powdered. Had to be heated to dissolve. Tasted like pencils.

We had meat once a week - usually on Sunday. Mom would kill one chicken for the 7 of us. Think there was 8 or 9 pieces. Not a lot - no seconds. Mom always ate the back. My sister and I drew straws to see who got the "pulley bone." Then we would break it into - the one that got the short piece had to wash dishes.

Thanks, Joy, for giving us such a poignant glimpse into the past.

17

Making margarine had evolved somewhat when I, as a little girl, was asked to help in the process. The white, soft, lard-looking stuff was now in a thick plastic package. There was a small capsule of coloring inside and my job was to push on the capsule until it released the yellow/orange colored liquid. Then I would massage the plastic package until all the liquid had been absorbed and it was the color of real butter. Then one end of the package would be cut off and the contents squeezed into round butter dishes, covered with wax paper, and put in the refrigerator to "set up."

Some Food for the Soul

Keep Your Face Toward the Sunshine and The Shadows Will Fall Behind You

You know folks, much of life is detemined by what you are looking at. I read in a book once about a man who always looked at the negative stuff in life. The author described him as someone who was always "looking for the rusty lining."

I'm sure you're not that kind of person—but if you're not careful, it's easy to get distracted by life's problems and forget life's possibilities.

A bunch of years ago I was at a conference where the theme was, "Look for the Good and Praise It!" You know—that's not a bad way to live. Since then I do my best to look for good in every area of life.

The trick is to stay alert for things to feel good about:

Look, there's a new purple flower near the sidewalk. It wasn't blooming yesterday. It showed up today just for me because purple is one of my favorite colors.

I'm not a Pollyanna—I see the guy whose driving is all over the place and whose fingers flashed me a sign (don't think it was the Peace sign) as he raced around my car. But I quickly try to notice that the other drivers are behaving themselves and keeping traffic flowing smoothly. So I make it a point to smile at them as they go by.

Each day I've found it helpful to quietly spend a few minutes being thankful for all the good there is in my life. Counting my blessings helps me to remember what's really important. So when a dark spot in life comes along, I can turn away from it more quickly and walk back into the light where I belong.

SECTION THREE

From
the
Garden

Garden Memories

My grandmother not only had a green thumb, she used it constantly. She and my grandfather loved planting things and seeing them grow, and so we had a large variety of garden goodies.

Even though my grandparents' house was in town, they had a very large lot behind the house, stretching halfway up the hill to the fence surrounding the baseball field. Grandfather had planted several rows of corn and pole beans. There were also potatoes, carrots, turnip greens, and kale. We were blessed with an abundance of fruit trees, including several large apple trees and a pear tree whose bounty was so heavy the limbs had to be propped up with large planks of lumber.

During World War II they planted a "Victory Garden" and increased the number of vegetables they could harvest and use, as well as providing fresh food to some of the less fortunate residents of our town.

Grandmother believed that she could grow anything, and she even had a couple of rows of strawberries—not what you would expect in the Blue Ridge Mountains of North Carolina. Her most ambitious experiment was the attempt to grow a producing lemon tree. Its beautiful waxy green leaves were delightful to see, but no lemons ever appeared. I think it might have had something to do with the fact that it had no other lemon trees to play with, an element my grandmother might not have considered.

I especially remember how delicious the fresh ears of corn were, and how wonderful they made grandmother's corn pudding taste. Add fried pork chops, a mess of turnip greens and fresh baked biscuits with sourwood honey and you've got real lickin' good eatin'!

Grandpa's Garden Salad
with Sweet Serendipity Vinaigrette

Candace McMenamin
Lexington, South Carolina

Ingredients:

1 Package (8 or 9 ounce) tortellini pasta
1 cup diced yellow squash (about 2 small)
1 cup diced zucchini (about 2 small)
½ cup diced sweet onion (preferably Vidalia)
1 cup diced, seeded, cucumbers
½ cup diced red or green sweet peppers
1 cup halved cherry tomatoes
2 cans (6 ounce) tuna packed in water, drained and chunked

Sweet Serendipity Vinaigrette:

2 large oranges
2 tablespoons granulated sugar
½ cup white wine vinegar
2 cloves garlic, minced

2 tablespoons snipped fresh dill
½ teaspoon black pepper
1 teaspoon salt
¼ cup vegetable oil

4 green lettuce leaves
Garnish: Dill sprigs and cherry tomato rosettes, if desired

Preparation:

Prepare tortellini according to package directions. Drain and rinse with cold water. Set aside until needed.

Combine yellow squash and next 5 ingredients in a 4-quart glass bowl. Add prepared tortellini. Lightly stir to mix. Gently fold in tuna. Set aside while preparing the vinaigrette.

Vinaigrette

Squeeze juice from the oranges into small glass bowl, removing any seeds. Add sugar, vinegar, garlic, dill, salt and pepper. Stir to combine. Gently whisk in oil. Pour vinaigrette over vegetable-tortellini salad mixture. Toss gently to coat. Refrigerate 30 minutes to meld the flavors.

To Serve

Place one lettuce leaf on each of 4 plates. Evenly divide salad among the four plates. Garnish with a dill sprig and cherry tomato rosettes, if desired.

Serves 4 (about 1 ¼ cups per serving)
Preparation time: 20 minutes
Refrigeration time: 30 minutes

 Lawsie mercy honey, you sho' done gone to a lot of trouble for this dish. But I admit my mouth was waterin' by the time I finished reading the recipe.

Behind the Recipe

Grandpa's Garden Salad
with Sweet Serendipity Vinaigrette

Happiness! This is what this recipe conjures up in my mind!

Watching Grandfather plan, plant, and then harvest his garden was such a joy. He loved gardening and involving all of the grandkids in the "chores."

Since I loved all the vegetables and wanted to showcase them in a recipe, I came up with this one and proudly presented the results to my grandfather. One taste and Grandpa declared it "Sweet Serendipity."

Candace McMenamin

Corn-off-the-Cob

Dotty Loop
St. Augustine, Florida

Ingredients:

6 - 8 ears of fresh corn - cleaned and de-silked

3 tablespoons of bacon grease

One-half stick of butter

½ teaspoon sugar

1 cup of water

Salt to taste

Iron skillet

Preparation:

With a sharp knife, slice the kernels of corn off the cobs and into a bowl. Scrape the juice from one or two cobs into the bowl. Add a cup of water.

On the side, heat up 3 tablespoons of bacon grease in an iron skillet. Pour the bowl of corn into the skillet. Cook for 15 minutes or so, stirring frequently.

Turn heat down to simmer and add ½ stick of butter. When melted, add ½ teaspoon of sugar and a little salt.

Cover skillet and let corn simmer for 20 minutes or so. If corn gets dry during cooking, add water.

4 - 6 Servings

My mother was an Alabama girl and an excellent cook, like her own mother. She married my father and moved to Florida. This was her recipe.

Once I fixed this for my crotchety father-in-law. He wolfed it down and said that it was the best corn he'd ever had. He was from Indiana. After that, he seemed to like me better.

 I'll have to agree with the judges who said that this was a "Very Mayberry" recipe!

Debbie's Coleslaw

Debbie Caruso
Clarksville, Tennessee

Ingredients:

Small head of cabbage

1 large or 2 small carrots

1 (firm and not juicy) tomato

Salt & pepper

3 heaping tablespoons mayonnaise

4 (pimento stuffed) green olives

½ green bell pepper - seeds and membrane removed

Preparation:

Using a hand-held shredder, shred cabbage and carrots into a medium-sized bowl. Cut off and throw away top of tomato, then cut tomato in half vertically. Shred the tomato into the mixture. When you get to the tomato skin, stop and toss that out. Cut and discard the top of the bell pepper and shred the remainder into the bowl. (The tomato and bell pepper will become very mushy and juicy when shredded.) Chop the olives into small pieces and add them to the mixture. Stir in mayonnaise. Add salt and pepper to taste. If it is too dry for you, you may add more mayonnaise.

Makes 4 or more servings, depending on how much folks like it.

This recipe started with cabbage and carrots when my grandma taught it to me. Over time, I changed it, adding things I thought would be good. People say to me, "What do you put in your slaw? It's different, but I love it."

Now, I only fix it on special occasions, or when my husband brings home that string of crappie, because it goes so well with those fish. Just like I use an iron skillet for cornbread, I use a manual shredder for slaw. Somehow, it just makes it better. Or maybe it just makes me think of days gone by—Mayberry Style.

Fried Green Tomatoes Olé

Evelyn M. Burgess
Siler City, North Carolina

Ingredients:

Oil for frying

¾ cup buttermilk

1¼ teaspoon salt

5 large green tomatoes, thinly sliced

2 jalapeno peppers, finely diced, seeds and membranes removed

4 eggs, beaten

½ cup cornmeal

2 cups flour

Preparation:

Combine eggs, buttermilk and salt. In a separate bowl, combine flour and cornmeal. Dip tomatoes into egg batter, then roll in flour mixture. Pour oil to about ¼ inch in a heavy frying pan. Fry tomatoes until golden brown.

In another small frying pan, add 1 tablespoon of oil. Sauté diced jalapeno peppers for 1 to 2 minutes over medium heat.

Sprinkle jalapeno peppers over fried green tomatoes.

Yields 6-8 servings.

My dad was an avid vegetable gardener. One of his favorite vegetables was pepper. He loved all the varieties, but especially hot ones. He had a habit he learned from his dad of keeping a jalapeno pepper beside his dinner plate. He would take a bite as needed to spice up a bland dish. Though he loved fried green tomatoes, he thought they needed some spice.

This recipe is a variation of his original. He ate his jalapenos raw and with seeds!

Would you believe that even though the chefs loved this recipe, they suggested the addition of crumbled bleu cheese on top? Talk about gilding the lily—or in this case, the tomato!

SECTION FOUR

More
Soul Food

The Amazing Power of Belief

"It is done unto you as you believe," the Good Book says, but I really found out what that can mean one evening many years ago in a nightclub in Hollywood, California.

Eight of us, friends from work and church, had come to see Pat Collins, billed as "The Hip Hypnotist." About halfway through her amazing and amusing performance, she came down into the audience. She approached our table and shortly convinced one of the young men in our group to come up on stage to be hypnotized.

After a little small talk, she began to put Roger "under." In a few minutes she took him to a wooden table and told him that it was a red-hot stove. I had seen people hypnotized before, so I wasn't surprised that when he touched the wooden table he screamed and jumped back, as if the surface had burned his hand. But when he came back to our table, we were really blown away by what we saw. Roger had blisters on his fingers! I mean, real blisters—just as if he *actually* burned his hand on a red-hot stove.

Well, I can guarantee you that the bunch of us talked about nothing else the rest of the evening. I didn't sleep very well that night wondering what in the world could have caused that to happen.

In the coming weeks and months I took it upon myself to do some research on the matter. I learned that people have been studying the connection between what we believe and what we experience for hundreds of years.

I'll spare you the encyclopedia version, but it seems that when we believe something deeply it helps bring about the thing we believe in. Now that can be a good thing. If we believe good things about ourselves, we're well on our way to experiencing those good things. But, on the other hand, if we believe negative things, we are actively pulling the rug out from under ourselves.

In Roger's case, his belief that he had put his hand on a hot stove sent the signals to his body, which produced the blisters, just as the real experience would have done. That really got my attention. I couldn't help but wonder what beliefs I might be holding on to that might be producing negative effects in my body.

Our bodies are designed with lots of automatic systems to keep us healthy. But we need to keep supporting those systems both physically and mentally.

It's important not to be afraid of getting an illness. Fear is the kind of emotion that "settles" in the subconscious mind and can act as a magnet for the thing feared.

For instance, put that TV remote on "Mute" the next time an ad comes on telling you that it's the "cold and flu season." Hogwash! Don't let advertising convince you that you are going to "catch" the most recent illness that is "going around." Instead, tell yourself that it will very easily "go around" you. When someone says, "Don't get too close to me, I don't want to give you my cold," I usually say, "That's OK. I'm infecting people with my health today."

How about it? Why not begin right now to use the amazing power of belief to bring a healthier and happier life into your experience!

Marvelous Meatloaf

Meatloaf and Mystery

*I*n the early years of marriage, I made meatloaf frequently. For one thing, it was relatively inexpensive, and, secondly, the "recipe" for it allowed for a good bit of creative license in the choosing of the ingredients. I can clearly remember what my new husband said one night as he sat down to a dinner featuring meatloaf.

"Oh, I see you cleaned out the refrigerator today!"

And he was right. Whatever vegetables were left over from previous meals were added to the ground meat, plus any stale bread that could be used to stretch the ingredients and make a larger loaf. The real test of the success of any particular meatloaf was the amount of ketchup he felt he needed to add to enjoy the offering.

My search for a "Marvelous Meat Loaf" brought many interesting entries. One mother admitted that the only way she could get vegetables into her children was to puree them and add them to her meatloaf.

However, the winner in this category added a special ingredient—love of her father. You know it's true—all the best recipes are prepared with love.

Dad's Meatloaf

Evelyn Burgess
Siler City, North Carolina

Ingredients:

2 pounds lean ground beef
2 large eggs
1 cup bread crumbs

1 teaspoon salt
¼ cup creamed corn

Salsa:

½ cup cilantro, chopped
3 ripe tomatoes, diced
¼ of a medium Vidalia onion, finely diced
½ cup mild green chilies, finely diced
1 tablespoon fresh lime juice
¼ teaspoon sugar

Preparation:

Preheat oven to 350 degrees.

Make salsa by combining and tossing the 6 ingredients. Divide in half.

In a large bowl, combine ground beef, eggs, bread crumbs, salt, creamed corn and half the salsa mixture. Mix ingredients until just blended.

In a 13 x 9-inch baking pan, shape meat mixture into a loaf. Bake uncovered for about 45 minutes. Remove from oven.

Top with remaining salsa mixture. Bake an additional 10 to 15 minutes or until done. Let stand 10 minutes before serving.

Makes 8 servings.

Behind the Recipe

Dad's Meatloaf

Though my dad has been gone for many years, he is still with me every day. So much of what I learned about cooking, and about life as well, was the result of his caring attention.

Born in 1917, he grew up on a small farm, and as a result spent more time in the fields than in the schoolroom. He joined the Army to get an education and help develop the skills he needed to succeed in life.

One of the main reasons he wanted to be able to read and write well was to study the Bible. He studied it so thoroughly that he virtually memorized it. I remember when I was growing up, if I was concerned about something, Dad would pull out of his memory bank a verse of scripture that would handle the matter perfectly.

In World War II Dad was a cook in the Army and was stationed in Europe. He was very interested in what people in other countries and cultures ate and how they prepared their food. He especially enjoyed learning about new ingredients from others he met while in service.

Dad had a very inquisitive mind and was open to new ideas. He was interested in what we now call "organic" foods way back in the '40s. He was interested in cooking with "wild" ingredients and knew which flowers and herbs were edible and which would be poison.

When he came back from the war he brought many new ideas on cooking and put them into practice at home. Growing his own vegetables and herbs added rich variety to his dishes.

When the Public Broadcasting Network came into being he faithfully watched all the cooking shows to hone his skills and expand his knowledge. This recipe is a variation of one of his many creative combinations for meatloaf.

Evelyn Burgess

Jean's Savory Stuffed Meatloaf

Wendy Nickel
Kiester, Minnesota

Ingredients:

Meatloaf

1½ pounds ground beef sirloin
½ cup dry Italian bread crumbs
2 eggs, beaten
1 teaspoon Worcestershire sauce
2 cloves garlic, minced
¼ teaspoon salt
⅛ teaspoon black pepper

Stuffing

⅓ cup pesto
1 cup mozzarella cheese, shredded

Topping

1 tomato, seeded and diced
2 tablespoons fresh basil, chopped
½ cup mozzarella cheese, shredded

Preparation:

Heat oven to 350 degrees.

In a large mixing bowl combine the beef with bread crumbs, eggs, Worcestershire sauce, garlic, salt and pepper.

On a piece of wax paper spread the meatloaf mixture in a 9 x 12 rectangle. Pat it evenly. Spread pesto and 1 cup of mozzarella cheese over the top. Roll up, starting at the short edge.

Place stuffed beef in a 9 x 5 inch loaf pan. Bake at 350 degrees for 50 - 60 minutes.

Mix topping ingredients together. Remove meatloaf from over and spread with topping. Return to oven for 5 minutes or until cheese melts.

Serves 8

Meatloaf—one of those comfort foods! This meatloaf recipe is named for my former music teacher. She lived close by, so I would ride my bike to her house when the weather was decent. I always remember that she would have supper cooking for her husband Ralph, so that when I finished my lesson they could eat supper.

Jean also told me that my parents were wasting their money on organ lessons because I had no talent. I still liked the woman—and knew she was right.

Chicken Cordon Bleu Saucy Mini-Meat Loaves

Candace McMenamin
Lexington, South Carolina

Ingredients:

1½ pounds ground chicken or turkey
½ cup grated carrots
1 small onion, chopped
2 eggs, beaten
1 cup Italian-flavored bread crumbs
1 (14.5 oz) can petite diced tomatoes, drained
6 oz. thinly sliced deli ham
6 oz. thinly sliced provolone cheese
1½ cups prepared spaghetti sauce
Garnish: parsley sprigs, if desired

Preparation:

Preheat oven to 350 degrees

In a large bowl, combine ground chicken, carrots, onion, eggs, bread-crumbs and tomatoes. Mix well. Shape into 6 equal mini-loaves.

Divide each loaf in half lengthwise. Evenly place ham and cheese on surface of bottom half of loaves. Replace top of loaves. Seal seams.

Place on a 15 x 10 baking pan that has been prepared with non-stick spray. Bake in oven for 45 minutes or until meat thermometer inserted in middle of loaves registers 160 degrees.

Heat spaghetti sauce in microwave safe bowl 2 minutes or until heated through.

Place loaves on serving platter and garnish with parsley sprigs, if desired. Have heated sauce available to pour over loaves, as desired.

Serves 6

I created this meatloaf recipe for all my "highfalutin" friends who think they have to have some fancy French food. I serve it up in an elaborate style and they don't even know they're eatin' meatloaf. I hear comments like, "Oh my dear, this is so divine," and "I must fix this for my next garden party!"

Shucks, it's just doctored up ole' meatloaf. But it tastes wonderful and is a breeze to make. I think Aunt Bee would be proud to serve it!

SECTION SIX

Even More
Soul Food

God Feeds the Birds of the Air
But He Does Not Drop the Worms Directly Into Their Mouths

When I was going to Sunday School at Central Methodist Church, I remember the teacher saying, "God has no hands but your hands His wondrous work to do." It was followed by a lesson on how, although God was providing many opportunities, we were expected to do our part to be successful in life and to contribute to the world. It was expressed more succinctly as "God helps those who help themselves."

Remember the wonderful character of Deputy Barney Fife that Don Knotts brought to life in *The Andy Griffith Show*? In interviews, Andy said that the show was never the same after Don left to do movies—that Don, as "Barney," was the heart of the show.

When the idea of a small town "Sheriff without a gun" was first shown on television, Sheriff Andy Taylor (played by Andy Griffith) and his son Opie (little Ronnie Howard) were incorporated into an episode of "The Danny Thomas Show." The response was so strong that a new television series with that focus was picked up immediately and scheduled for airing in the fall of 1960.

Shortly after "The Danny Thomas Show" episode aired, Don Knotts called his old friend, Andy Griffith, (they'd worked together on Broadway in *No Time For Sergeants*) to congratulate him on the upcoming TV series. Then Don, who was at that time "between jobs," said to Andy, "Don't you think the show would be even better if you had a Deputy. And how about if the Deputy was me?" The rest is humor history!

Deputy Barney Fife might never have happened if Don Knotts hadn't been willing to speak up for himself. Are you reluctant to speak up? Are you afraid to move forward to grasp opportunities?

The Master Teacher Jesus taught, "Knock and it shall be opened unto you." He didn't tell you to just stand there and hope something drops into your lap. He said, "Ask, and it shall be given unto you."

So…What are you waiting for?

SECTION SEVEN

Down Memory Lane

Milkshakes and Memories

"Jew-ell, time for be-edd," my mother singsonged from the stairs.

"Can't I stay up a little longer?" I pleaded. Grandfather said I could help him make his milkshake."

"I'll make sure she gets to bed directly, Mabel. She won't be long," Grandfather replied, winking at me. We were known for stretching our time together.

"All right, but remember, she's got school in the morning."

In the kitchen, Grandfather handed me the small metal grater and a dark brown nutmeg. "I'll need about a teaspoon-full," he said, "and be careful of your fingers." Cautiously I scraped the nutmeg against the rough edges of the grater, delighted to be entrusted with a vital part of the special recipe.

Grandfather went over to the Hamilton-Beach mixer and removed the tall silver-toned cup. I had often wondered just how many milkshakes this wonderful machine had prepared. It had been a fixture of the soda fountain in the Creed Book Store for many years.

My grandfather had come back to Mount Airy from Roanoke, Virginia a number of years ago to take over the bookstore business after his brother, Will, had died. In those days, all the high school students had to buy their books, and the State of North Carolina had designated our family bookstore for the purchases in this area. The store also carried cigarettes, cigars, stationery, and additional sundry items for the grown-ups. But it was the wonderful milkshakes, sundaes, and other such goodies that kept the place crowded with young people.

The Creed Book Store was no longer in operation, but the mixer, more than a foot tall, with a heavy white ceramic base, still was. Only now it was operating from a place of honor in our kitchen, faithfully churning out Grandfather's daily concoction.

When the milkman from Surry Dairy delivered four glass bottles to the front door every other morning, Grandmother knew exactly how to handle them before putting them in the Kelvinator refrigerator. Each had a two-inch layer of cream positioned in the neck of the bottle. One bottle she would turn side to side and then rotate completely, to make sure all the cream was mixed in. She would skim half the cream off the two other bottles, saving it in another container for whipped cream or other delights. The last bottle she placed in the refrigerator on the top shelf on the right side. It was set aside for Grandfather and when the time came for it to be used in his special milkshake, then, and only then, would he, and only he, decide how much cream would go into the mixture.

This night he removed the bottle and, with reckless abandon, poured *all* the cream into the milkshake container and followed it with half of the bottle of milk, leaving the remainder of milk to fend for itself. Then he took an egg from the carton, tapped it on the side of the counter and, with one smooth move, deftly opened the shell and deposited the raw egg into the milk. Next came the sugar, scooped from the green hobnail glass jar with no apparent measurement. A dash of vanilla from a bottle in the cupboard followed.

"Go ahead, Jewell, put the nutmeg in." he said, and with the flourish of an honored chef, I sprinkled the aromatic shavings on the top of the mixture.

Soon the metal cup was positioned on the stand engaging the motor and initiating the whirring of the stirrer as it did its magic on the mix.

"Got your glass, Jewell? It won't take long." Grandfather said, unable to disguise his excitement. Although making his milkshake was a regular routine, he always acted as if it was a once-in-a-lifetime treat.

Grandfather removed the milkshake cup and began to pour a small serving into my glass. Momentarily, the thought of raw egg caused me to feel queasy, but the joy of sharing my grandfather's pleasure overcame any other ideas.

As both of us sipped and smiled, Grandfather said, "Don't forget, Jewell, a milkshake a day keeps the doctor away."

The phrase sounded somewhat familiar—but I wasn't sure. But then, nothing really mattered but sipping and sharing with my grandfather.

Saturday Supper

Sometimes it's not the food, but the circumstances under which it is served, that make the memories so tasty.

Mine was a single mom, working full time and raising a young daughter. The significant support (both financial and physical) of her parents was a great help, but due to her schedule, I spent the great majority of the time at my grandparents' house. I would go there after school. When Mother got off work she'd meet me there, and we'd all eat supper together. By the time Mother and I went home to the apartment we shared, it was my bedtime.

But most Saturdays Mother and I spent the day alone together. And the routine for the evening meal that day rarely varied. Mother would set up the card table, with a nice cotton tablecloth covering it, in the living room near the radio. The Saturday night programs were a shared enjoyment. So we would always eat while listening to, and looking at, the radio.

My mother acknowledged that cooking was just not her strong suit and so the food she served was simple, but filling.

In the winter we would have a hearty soup, the ingredients for which had been carefully selected and prepared by Campbell's. To the side would be a sandwich made with white bread, crusts removed. Duke's mayonnaise would be generously spread on the bread and a slice of luncheon meat, perhaps "spiced ham," would make up the sandwich. A glass of sweet milk and a cup of hot tea completed the offering.

The casual setting did not in any way relieve me of my obligation to watch my manners. When Mother felt an infraction had occurred, she did not hesitate to reach over and turn down the radio in order to make sure I understood her correction. Not wanting to miss a moment of "Gene Autry's Melody Ranch," I was careful to watch my p's & q's.

Then, if I had been a good girl and eaten all my supper (remembering that there were little children starving in Armenia who would have been glad to have what I had been served) the "treat" would be brought out.

The familiar dark brown rounds with the stark white filling were always a welcome sight. Date nut bread with cream cheese! My favorite! Straight out of the Crosse and Blackwell can, 2 thick slices of date nut bread with Philadelphia cream cheese (mixed with little milk to make it spread better) in between. YUMMY!

Of course, it all tasted better because my mother was eating the same food as I was, and in that magical time, giving me her full attention.

Oh yes, supper on Saturday was always special!

Food and Friendship

The buying of groceries surely has changed dramatically since I was young, and not all for the better, from my point of view.

Today, we order "online" from Omaha Steaks hundreds of miles away for our beef needs. The meat may be fine, but something is missing in the method.

When I was growing up my grandmother called the local butcher at Stewart's Meat Market to see what they had that day that was "good."

"Do your have any tenderized ham?" Grandmother would ask.

"Oh yes, Mizz Creed," the butcher would reply.

"But is it really tender?" She would press, not willing to trust an advertising spiel.

"I'll make sure you get the best slices, Mizz Creed."

"Well then, I'll take a pound."

"Mighty fine, Mizz Creed. We'll send it right out to you."

And it arrived at our door that afternoon, fresh and delicious.

Most of our regular grocery purchases were made at Poore's Grocery Store on

Main Street which was owned by distant cousins. A fixture in Mount Airy, North Carolina for almost 60 years, Poore's was the epitome of a small town grocery that delivered both food and friendship.

Founded by Floyd Poore in 1891, when I was growing up it was being run by his son, Walter, and his wife, Doris. I never ran out of things to see in that store. Every inch of space was taken up with appealing displays and aromatic delights.

One of the real treats for me was when Cousin Walter would let me go into the back room to watch the other employees "candle" eggs. They called it that, because in the past candles had been used in the process. Now each egg was held up to a bare light bulb, which let you look through the thin eggshell and check to see if the yolk was alright. He explained that they were making sure there were no clots of blood around the yolk, or a cloudy look to the egg white that would mean that the egg wasn't good. Once in awhile, he would let me hold an egg in front of the light bulb. "Well, what do ya think, Jewell—is that one fit to eat?" After a while I learned to pick out the bad ones easily, and it was a skill I was very proud of.

Grandfather loved dill pickles. As soon as we got in the grocery store, he would head for the pickle barrel and select a plump juicy one, munching on it as we picked out items to be added to our written order, which would later be delivered to the house. When Cousin Doris tallied up the total to be added to our family's charge account, Grandfather would always say, "Now, Doris, don't forgit to add on that de-licious pickle I just et."

Doris would smile and say, "I don't rightly think I see a pickle, Judge Creed, and I can't charge you for something I don't see."

"Much obliged." With a smile and a nod, Grandfather would lick his lips, pat his stomach, and the ritual would be complete.

During my years at Rockford Street Grammar School, I went almost every day to the grocery store to pick up bread or some other small item for my mother or grandparents. Each time I would get myself a nickel candy bar and have it added to the order.

After many months of this routine, one day when Doris was totaling up the items, she turned to me and very pleasantly asked, "Jewell, does your mother know you are buying a candy bar every day?"

I took a deep breath and tried to appear unconcerned. "I don't know if she does or not. I'm not sure I have mentioned it to her." I hoped my voice didn't betray the shaking I felt inside my body.

"Well, honey, she might not want you to have that much candy; it's not really good for your teeth, you know. You might want to check with her before you buy any more." Doris continued to smile as she packed the items in a small brown sack.

"Yes, Ma'am, I will." I grabbed the sack and got out of there as fast as I could. Doris and my mother were good friends and talked frequently. I really hoped she wouldn't say anything to Mother before I got a chance.

I mulled over the situation as I walked very slowly down South Main Street, past the high school, turning at the Presbyterian Church and down the Church Street hill to my grandparents' home. Mother would be there soon. I didn't want to tell her. I was afraid to tell her, but Cousin Doris wouldn't let me have any more candy until I gave her an okay from Mother. I tried to find a good time to talk with Mother that evening after we had gotten back to our apartment, but I never could get the words out of my mouth.

I avoided going back to Poore's for several days. When I finally did, I walked in, picked up a loaf of bread, took it to the clerk to be thin-sliced, and then, acting as casually as I could manage, brought the bread over to Cousin Doris at the counter.

"Well, hello, Jewell. I haven't seen you around the past few days. By the way, how's your Mother doing these days?" Doris tipped her head and displayed her ever-present smile.

I answered her using my strongest, brightest voice, accompanied by my best Shirley Temple grin. "Oh, she's fine, Mizz Poore. And by the way, I asked her about my charging a candy bar every day, and she agrees with you that it probably wouldn't be good for my teeth. She says 3 candy bars a week should be enough for me to have. I think I'll take an Almond Joy today, if you please."

Walking home, I tried to swallow the "story" with the candy. The chocolate and nuts were *delicious*! And so, I found out years later, was the laughter between my mother and Doris, who had the operator ring Mother on the phone as soon as I left the store.

Although by the mid-forties large grocery chains such as Kroger, A & P and Piggly-Wiggly had moved onto Main Street, with advertising specials, shopping carts, and "low prices," Poore's Grocery remained in business until 1950, when Walter Poore's health finally caused the closing of the store and the ending of an era.

Nuts and Spices

*P*reparations for the Thanksgiving and Christmas holidays began early at Grandmother's house. Dark, rich, moist fruitcakes were made at the beginning of October. Large round pans were used for family cakes and loaf pans for gifts. Since I was designated to stir the batter with the big wooden spoon, my hands and arms would be quite tired and aching at the end of a day of baking duties. But I tried not to complain. It was an important part of a honored ritual.

"Mix it in better, Jewell. Make sure you can't see any flour," Grandmother instructed. All the flour, molasses, candied citron, cherries and pecans were folded in and stirred carefully until the mixture developed into an appropriately stiff batter.

Preparation for some of the ingredients was done even earlier in the year. When the pecan crop came in from the groves on her tenant farms, Grandmother, Mother, and I would sit down with a bucket full of pecans, armed with nutcrackers and shiny picks ready for action. We cracked the pecan shells carefully in order to get the pecan halves out whole for fruitcakes and other fancy baked goods. The crisp, aromatic halves were carefully put in a covered glass jar and saved for their divine purposes. Any broken pieces were put in another container to be used in candy, brownies, and other baking that didn't require the perfection of intact halves.

A dozen or so fruitcakes were made in the course of a day. The delicious aroma of fruit and spices permeated the entire house, and wafted out the kitchen windows, alerting the neighborhood to the delights within. It was not surprising that the other children on the street chose this time to come over to see if I could come out to play.

Grandmother always refused the request, explaining, "Jewell can't come out now—she's helpin' with the baking." I would swell with pride at her words. I could play anytime - being trusted to help Grandmother was much more important. However, each neighbor child would be allowed to linger in the kitchen long enough to go away with at least one piece of cake that "didn't come out quite right."

When the cakes were removed from the oven, Grandmother placed fresh cut apple slices around the outsides and into the center holes. Honey-glazed and cooled, they were then wrapped in wax paper and placed in various cake tins and other containers for storage in the cellar underneath the house. "They need time for the flavors to marry," Grandmother stated, her voice resonating with years of experience.

By the time Thanksgiving came 'round, the apple slices had fermented and the juices and flavor seeped into the fruitcakes, giving them a tinge of alcohol not otherwise permitted in Grand-mother's teetoataling household.

Other designated baking days would produce additional goodies, among them banana nut bread, apple and prune loaves, and pumpkin spice bread. One of my favorites was a black walnut bread, although I certainly didn't relish the preparations for it. The walnuts came from a very large tree outside the back porch door. Mother Nature had devised an effective protection for the tree's delicious product. First was a tough covering of black and green, almost like leather. Touching it immediately produced a stain on the fingers and on anything else they subsequently touched. Consequently, the effort to harvest the delicious meat of this nut was relegated to the backyard.

Once its external guarding peel was removed, wearing pairs of Grandmother's old gardening gloves to protect our hands, the second layer of protection was exposed—an extremely hard and rough black shell. No nutcrackers were up to this task. We would place each shell on the concrete sidewalk and, holding it tightly with the left hand, use a sturdy hammer to strike it with the right hand. I was less than skillful at this task, and had a number of bruised fingers to attest to my inadequacies.

One year, a great idea came to me, and saved me from further embarrassment and pain. Placing my small red wooden chair on the sidewalk, I pulled the bucket of fresh black walnuts to my side and took my place on the chair. One by one, I placed those rough, hard-shelled nuts between my two feet, being careful to wear old, but sturdy, shoes. Using my feet as a vise, I pounded away until each shell split open and gave up its bounty.

Occasionally, Grandfather was enlisted for this important project. I watched in awe as he broke open each black walnut swiftly with a single blow of his hammer. My job was to quickly pick the nut sections up and put them in a bucket so the women could remove their contents later.

There was no effort by any of the participants in these violent nut-killing scenes to keep the black walnut meat unbroken. Pieces of black walnuts were just fine for cakes, breads and dark, delicious fudge.

Each time I began to tire, I kept my efforts going by anticipating enjoying delicious black walnut bread, warm, sweet and freshly buttered, together with my mother's special hot, spiced tea.

My mother prided herself on her spiced tea recipe. It was hot, strongly-brewed black pecoe tea with the addition of orange and pineapple juices and cloves, simmered for "just the right amount of time." She called it "Russian Tea," and served it for all the ladies' bridge functions, together with white bread sandwiches carefully cut in the shapes of clubs, diamonds, hearts and spades.

Imagine my surprise many years later, when I was living in the Kingdom of Saudi Arabia, and a Middle Eastern friend of mine served a tea made by the exact same recipe, proudly describing it as "my mother's special recipe for Sudanese Tea."

While I was growing up, Grandmother was adamant that "no store-bought fruitcake is as good as homemade." However, in the mid 1940's when a Kroger supermarket opened in Mount Airy, and my grandmother was pushing 80, she told everybody that she had tasted Kroger's fruitcake and it would be satisfactory. Her Holiday Baking Spoon was retired and we purchased our fruitcakes from that time on.

The Snappy Lunch

*a*s I got out of my car in the parking lot, I smelled the delicious aroma of food cooking at the Snappy Lunch. It smelled just like it did when I was a little girl going there with my grandfather.

When you open the screen door at the place, you step back in time. There is a simple menu, no frills, low prices and an open, welcoming atmosphere. Yes-siree, this is the famous Snappy Lunch.

It wasn't famous when I used to eat there with my grandfather. Well, actually it *was* famous with all the townspeople of Mount Airy and the surrounding area. The restaurant began serving its delicious offerings in 1923, and when I went there in the 1940's, it was *the* place to eat breakfast or lunch.

George Roberson, who was one of Grandfather's neighbors on Church Street, was one of the original owners, and my grandfather took every opportunity to support his friend's business. Not that it took much effort; the food was delicious and the conversation enlightening.

In the beginning, patrons stood at the counter to eat. When I was going there with Grandfather, they had added stools at the counter, and a few high school desks for seating. I would slide into one of the desks to eat my juicy hot dog while my grandfather "chewed the fat" with Mr. Roberson. In those days they had sandwiches for 5 and 10 cents, and nothing was over 20 cents.

All those memories came flooding back as I settled into a seat at the Snappy Lunch recently. The establishment now had seating for 40 people, having taken over the adjacent Fant's Shoe Repair, adding booths in that area.

Andy Griffith remembered his time at the Snappy Lunch also, and mentioned it on *The Andy Griffith Show,* spreading its reputation for good food and good conversation far and wide.There are many interesting pictures on the walls, but two caught my particular attention. The first was of Charles Dowell, the owner and Oprah Winfrey; the second was of the naked back of a rabid fan who had all the major characters on the show *tattooed* on his back.

The Snappy Lunch is busy virtually all of the time from its opening at 6 a.m. to the 2 p.m closing time. You're more likely to encounter local people at breakfast. They've pretty well given up being able to eat in the place at lunch time, settling for calling in their orders for "take out."

The day I ate lunch there there was a big bunch of people standing at the front waiting for their orders, and the waitresses seemed to know them all personally.

"Bob, your order for 19 tenderloin biskits is ready," Dorothy called out.

Bob moved to the front of the group of about 15 people waiting for similar orders. Some of the orders were breakfast items with a twist: "I got 7 sausage sandwiches with tomato and mayo—I think that's yours, Elmer."

The Snappy Lunch is owned by Charles Dowell, who began working there in 1943, sweeping and cleaning up in the place. My conversation with him revealed many of the reasons, in addition to good food, that the place is so popular.

"We served white bread when we opened and we serve white bread now. Why mess with anything else? Keepin' it simple is part of the secret, and simple is what I grew up with," Charles explained.

For all of us who have seen the huge tractor trailer trucks pull up to our favorite restaurants and unload the pre-processed food ingredients to be used in the restaurant's meals, you will be interested in the way the Snappy Lunch prepares its food.

"We make all our own chili—our own slaw—our own batter. Nothing we serve is processed anywhere else. We do it ourselves. They bring in the raw meat we cut and batter the pieces."

For a number of years now, the Snappy Lunch has been famous for its pork chop sandwich. You can get it regular or "all the way." When I asked what "all the way" meant, Charles looked at the waitress and said, "Go ahead, Dorothy, tell her what it means—it won't make any difference, she'll order it "all the way." I did—the statistics are that 99 out of 100 order it that way. (It includes tomato, onion, mustard, chili, and slaw, and produces a sandwich which is very difficult to handle and impossible to eat daintily—but who cares?)

Charles asked a sign maker to craft a sign saying that they served a pork chop sandwich to put on the outside of the restaurant. When the sign arrived, it said, "Home of the Famous Pork Chop Sandwich."

Charles said, "I told him I wish he hadn't done that, because it looked like I was braggin' and that ain't seemly."

"That very week a North Carolina television station came to do a story on the Snappy Lunch and they zoomed in on that sign, and once the story ran, it created a great demand. What really put us over the top was when the people from the Oprah Winfrey Show came here and asked about the pork chop sandwich, and it got mentioned on her show. They really put us on the map."

Also, it's not every day a pork chop sandwich gets written up in *Gourmet* Magazine:

"It takes more than a glorified pork chop in a hamburger bun
to generate the kind of allure radiated by this diner on Main

Street. Snappy Lunch serves each of its customers a generous helping of small-town America—and that is a tasty dish that's getting mighty hard to find."

—*Gourmet*

On an ordinary day, at least 200 pork chop sandwiches are sold, and many, many more during "Mayberry Days." At $3.65, the pork shop sandwich is the most expensive thing on the lunch menu. Charles is very proud of his affordable prices.

"You don't see other eating places with these kind of prices. I know I could get more; there's no doubt that I could almost double my prices and they'd still keep coming. But that's not the right way. I like to see people happy. I think one of the things I was impressed with growing up was that in this town people try to help each other, not take advantage of each other."

He's certainly right about the prices. At the Snappy Lunch a family of four, all eating cheeseburgers, chugging down sodas and sharing two packages of potato chips, would owe a grand total of $12.10. Take that McDonalds!

You won't find dessert on the menu, but if you must have something sweet to finish your lunch, you can choose from individual servings of goodies displayed in the original Lance boxes used for shipping. You could choose cookies, small pecan or chess pies or a "Fat Free Fig Cake."

When asked what he liked best about his job, Charles replied, "The most fun part of the job is seeing people you'd never see otherwise, listening to them, seeing them laughing together—how excited they are to be here—helping them reconnect with the past."

They don't call it "Snappy Lunch" for nothing. The food is served hot and quick; true fast food with an "all the time in the world" feeling for the customer. In spite of lines out the door, no one is ever rushed. Here people really *are* more important than profits.

The Snappy Lunch is fast, frugal and fantastic. If you're up Mount Airy way, come on in—the people are friendly and the vittles are great!

Famous Pork Chop Sandwich

Charles Dowell
Owner, Snappy Lunch
Mount Airy, North Carolina

Ingredients:

12 large boneless pork chops
Cooking grease

Batter:

2 cups of plain (not self-rising) flour
2 tablespoons of sugar
2 eggs
Salt to taste
1 cup sweet milk (more or less)

Preparation:

Pound the pork chops with a tenderizer.

To make the batter—in a large mixing bowl mix flour, sugar, eggs and salt.

Add milk gradually and beat the mixture until the batter is very smooth. It is important to make sure it is not lumpy—but also not watery. (Test by dipping a spoon into the batter. If the batter runs off the spoon, you can be sure it will run off the pork chop, and you want it to stick to it.)

Get the grease in the skillet hot—but not hot enough to scorch the batter. The goal is to get the pork chops cooked through and looking brown, but not burned.

Dip the pork chops into the batter until they have a generous covering and put them on the skillet. Don't rush the process. Chops need to be cooked well. Turn them occasionally.

To serve them the Snappy Lunch way—place on steamed buns with mustard, homemade chili, homemade slaw, chopped onions, and sliced tomato.

P.S. Charles says that a slightly thinner batter is great for onion rings!

Neither Andy Griffith nor I had the opportunity to eat this delicious sandwich at the Snappy Lunch while we were growing up. It came along much later. But I certainly have had the opportunity to munch down on this flavorful offering in more recent years.

Regional TV Channel 4 in Jacksonville, Florida asked me to come on their Morning Show and cook and serve the pork chop sandwich to the anchors and crew. When I arrived at the studio I met the Weatherman, Richard Nunn, whom I had been watching and enjoying for some time.

He told me that he was from Ararat, Virginia only a few miles from Mount Airy, N.C. Then it hit me. Andy Griffith's mother's maiden name was Geneva Nunn; and sure enough, Richard was a part of her extended family.

And to top it off—Richard had eaten the Famous Pork Chop Sandwich at the real Snappy Lunch.

Talk about being on the spot!! But my pork chop sandwiches disappeared quickly and the cast and crew of the TV station were very generous with their compliments.

This recipe is trickier than it looks. It's that dratted and delicious batter that'll get you. It has to be just right. But if you're bound and determined to give it a try—have at it!

My recommendation is that you go to Mount Airy, N.C. in September during Mayberry Days (when they celebrate The Andy Griffith Show) and get yourself a Famous Pork Chop Sandwich prepared by the one and only Charles Dowell himself!

SECTION EIGHT

Soups
and Stews

Hearty and Healthy

*H*earty—filling—yummy! Those are the words that describe the flavorful bowls of tasty ingredients that appeared on our dining room table in the winter months. Sometimes requiring extended cooking periods, their mouthwatering aromas would waft through the whole house, bringing me to the kitchen again and again to see if they were "ready" yet.

My very favorite was what my grandmother just called "Bean Soup." It was a delicious concoction of white navy beans simmered with a ham hock. By the time it was served, some of the beans had disintegrated, adding body to the soup and making it very filling. A large bowl of Bean Soup with a generous serving of corn bread, freshly baked in an iron skillet, was a supper from heaven for me.

My grandfather's favorite was Oyster Stew, and only because I loved him so much, did I learn to consume it with its squishy ingredients.

Like much of the "comfort" food served in the South, recipes for favorite soups and stews are sometimes hard to pin down. Each cook adds to and subtracts from whatever recipe has been handed down to her, in order to suit the tastes of her particular family members.

Take these great recipes and make them your own.

Aromatic Baked Potato Soup

Lisa Hurst
Blacksburg, Virginia

Ingredients:

½ pound thick cut smoked bacon, diced

4 large "baking" potatoes, scrubbed, peeled and sliced into thin rounds

4 cups chicken stock

2 cups whole buttermilk

1 cup Half and Half or cream

1 cup sour cream

2½ cups hoop cheese, shredded (Any mild cheddar or Colby can be used. If you use very sharp cheeses, substitute sweet milk for buttermilk.)

¾ cup ramp tops (green part only) finely chopped [Ramps, or wild leeks, are becoming harder to find fresh in certain areas; dried ramps may be purchased in gourmet stores (use ½ as much dry as fresh) or scallions may be substituted (use 1½ cups or more to taste)]

Salt & coarse ground pepper

Preparation:

In the bottom of a large, sturdy stew pot cook the diced bacon until it begins to brown, but do not let it become "crispy." Pour off the extra fat, to taste; it is best with about ¼ cup of the bacon fat in the pot.

Add sliced potatoes to bacon in stew pot; cover completely with chicken stock, and boil on medium-high heat until the potatoes become just soft enough to break with a fork; do not let the potatoes overcook and become mushy.

With a potato masher, break up the cooked potatoes to a chunky consistency. Do not cream or mash them, as they should retain nice bits of whole potato for texture.

Add buttermilk and reduce soup to low-medium heat. Gradually stir in Half and Half and sour cream. Slowly add grated cheese, stirring constantly and gently, until the cheese blends without becoming clumpy. Add ramps and salt and coarse ground pepper to taste.

Reduce heat, and simmer on very low heat 10 minutes. Avoid boiling the soup again before serving or reheating, as it will change the texture.

Serve hot with fresh bread or biscuits.

Serves 6 - 8

Behind The Recipe

Aromatic Baked Potato Soup

Several years ago, after moving into our new home together in south-western Virginia, my husband and I had our first big newlywed spat. Afterward, my husband went to "cool off" on a hike in the Cascade Mountains, on the border of West Virginia, not far from our new house. It was a good choice; we both needed the time and I settled down to burn off some energy setting up our new kitchen.

He was gone for most of the day and, when he returned, he stuck his head in the door with one hand hidden behind his back, and leaned in the kitchen door for a kiss.

"He's got wildflowers!" I thought, a romantic truce. As I shoved aside boxes and approached him with a pucker, I inhaled an odor like high noon at a mid-August garlic merchant's.

I jumped back flapping and gasping as a rustic wind of onion and garlic emanated from his lips, filling the small kitchen. "What on EARTH have you eaten?" I winced, covering my mouth and nose.

With a laugh, he held out his surprise "bouquet" of ramps. "Wild onions! They're called "ramps" and I found them in a field near the state line. Here! They're good. I tried them!" he coaxed. I was dubious, but it was a peace offering, smelly or not.

That night, I chopped a few of the ramps and put them in his favorite dish—my Baked Potato Soup - instead of my usual leeks. To my surprise, it lent a wonderful, woodsy, robust flavor that was better than my standard recipe.

That evening, our bouquet of wild "flowers" made the perfect truce, the perfect soup . . . and a perfect (and mutually aromatic) conciliatory kiss.

Lisa Hurst

Raving About Ramps!

Lisa Hurst
Blacksburg, Virginia

In the years since my first introduction to "ramps" I have learned of the deep history of ramps in the Appalachian region—its many nutritional, medicinal and culinary uses, dating back to (and before) the first English settlers who came to this region.

Interestingly, it seems the word "ramps" evolved from the early settlers' Old English word for a similar wild English garlic plant. The plant grew only in the weeks under the astrological sign of the "Ram"; hence (some think) the North American wild onion was named for its English cousin and their zodiac constellation.

Well before English settlement, regional Native American tribes used ramps for food, as bee sting poultices, and for colds. However, they celebrated its pungency with the name "skunk weed."

In our own time, small towns throughout the Appalachian Mountains annually celebrate the ramp and its history. During the plant's brief growing season, from April to May, many communities host "Ramp Festivals" such as the "Graham County Annual Ramp Festival" in North Carolina. There are numerous other festivals in the Appalachian region. These are updated regularly on devoted ramp Websites on the Internet. Just search for "Ramps."

Ramp Festivals are held in the Spring in North Carolina, Virginia, Tennessee and West Virginia. It is estimated that 3,200 pounds of ramps are used in these festivals.

According to National Geographic, the only one known ramp farm is in West Virginia. They sell fresh ramps in season, as well as seeds and bulbs for growing your own. All other harvesting is done in the wild. The Great Smoky Mountains National Park has now banned all ramp harvests there. If you have a hankering to cook with ramps, I wish you a happy, smelly experience.

Momma's Meatball Stew

Kathy Dvornick
St. Augustine, Florida

Ingredients:

12 meatballs (recipe follows)
2 8 ounce cans of tomato sauce
¼ cup each diced onion, celery and carrots
1 clove garlic, minced
4 large all purpose potatoes, cubed
1 package frozen peas
⅛ cup dry red wine or water
Salt and pepper to taste
Olive oil (just enough to cover the bottom of a large pot)
1 cup water

Meatballs

¾ pound ground beef
¼ pound ground pork
¾ cup bread crumbs (moistened with milk)
2 eggs, beaten
1 tablespoon fresh minced parsley or 1/2 teaspoon dry
1 clove minced garlic
¼ cup olive oil
Salt and pepper to taste

Meatball Preparation:

In a large bowl, mix meat, bread crumbs, eggs, parsley, garlic, salt and pepper. Form into balls.

In a large skillet heat olive oil. Cook meatballs over medium heat until well browned on all sides. Remove from pan and drain on paper towel to absorb excess oil.

Makes about 12 meatballs.

Stew Preparation:

Place olive oil in pan. When oil is hot sauté celery, onions, carrots and garlic about 3 minutes. Do not allow the garlic to burn, as it will taste bitter. Add the tomato sauce and wine (if using) and the cup of water.

Bring to a boil, add cubed potatoes and meatballs, and lower the heat. Simmer until potatoes are almost done. Then add frozen peas and continue cooking until potatoes are tender and peas are cooked.

Serves 6

Growing up my grandmother was my special friend. She lived with us and was my caregiver while my Mom and Dad worked. It was my greatest pleasure to sit on the edge of the kitchen counter while "Momma" prepared our evening meal. She had a knack for creating original recipes and her meatball stew was the best. Oh! How I cherish those memories.

Now, I am the grandmother and my darling granddaughter, Julianna, sits on my counter watching me.

Creamy Potato Soup With Okra Dumplings

Cheryl Perry
Elizabeth City, North Carolina

Ingredients:

Soup

3 cups potatoes, cubed
1 quart vegetable stock
2 cups heavy cream
¼ cup all purpose flour
¼ cup melted butter
2 cups heavy cream

1 teaspoon salt
1 teaspoon pepper
1 teaspoon onion powder
1 teaspoon garlic powder
1 teaspoon thyme

Dumplings

1 cup frozen okra, chopped
1½ cups all purpose flour
1 egg, beaten
¼ teaspoon salt
¼ teaspoon pepper
½ cup milk

Preparation:

In a large covered pot cook potatoes in salted water until fork tender. Mash the potatoes well and set aside.

To a large Dutch oven add the melted butter and sprinkle ¼ cup flour;

stir together and cook for 3 minutes over medium heat. Add the vegetable stock and cream; bring to a simmer and cook for 10 minutes or until thickened.

Meanwhile make the dumplings by blending together the flour, egg, salt and pepper. Add the okra, then milk, a small amount at a time, until dumpling mix comes together without being dry.

Bring pot to a simmer once more, then drop dumplings into simmering soup by tablespoonfuls. Recover pot tightly and continue to simmer for 15 minutes or until center of dumpling is no longer moist.

Turn off heat and re-season, if necessary.

Makes 4-6 servings

Cream based soups are my favorites to eat and to make. Okra is the only vegetable (besides a salad or green beans) my daughter will eat, so I've added them into the dumplings in this recipe.

This version is vegetarian, but the flavor can be enhanced with other stocks and/or meat additions.

Stella Mary's Soul-Satisfying Vegetable Soup

Lucy B. Holmes
Whitehall, Montana

Ingredients:

8 ounces Navy or Northern beans

1 medium onion, finely chopped

2 stalks of celery, chopped

1 medium carrot, chopped

1 can (14.5 oz) tomatoes (stewed or diced)

1 clove of garlic, minced (or 1 teaspoon of prepared chopped garlic)

1 tablespoon of basil

Salt and Pepper to taste

Oil to cover bottom of cooking pot

Preparation:

Soak beans overnight. Drain before adding to mixture the next day.

Put oil in large Dutch Oven. Heat until hot, but not sizzling. Add onion, celery and carrot and cook until onion is translucent.

Add tomatoes, garlic, and basil and mix. Add drained beans and enough water to cover. Bring to a boil and then reduce heat to simmer. Cover, leaving a small opening for steam to escape. Cook for 1 1/2 to 2 hours until beans are soft. If necessary, add more water during the cooking period.

This is a full-hearty soup and is delicious accompanied by crusty bread. It will warm and fill your empty tummy, and make your soul sing "Hallelujah!"

Makes 12 servings

Back in the depression years, we six children were lucky to have a mother who could, as it is often said, get flavor out of a rock. Times were hard. There was no work, which translated into no money. Struggling proud people, who had always made their own way, stood in soup lines and were grateful for the handout.

Momma honed her culinary skills by using what was available, and the faithful standby "make-do." We were living in Charleston, South Carolina and I remember the melodic Gullah sounds of the street vendors pushing their rickety carts down our street. This is where, after a pleasant back and forth bargaining session, that Stella Mary procured what she would turn into a culinary delight and all would eat.

Stella Mary was entitled to be her cantankerous self, but never did any distasteful measure of her misgivings transfer to her food and never did she give us her recipes. They could only be gotten by stealth and practice. Disguised as a sack of potatoes, I managed to procure this Soul-Satisfying Vegetable Soup!

SECTION NINE

More
Soul Food

What's Got Your Attention?

Do your problems get all your attention?

Problems don't go away because you're thinking about them. In fact, it's just the opposite. If I'm worrying and fussing about something, it takes over more and more of my energy. And wouldn't you know it—things not only don't get better - they usually get worse.

The more attention and emotion you give a problem, the more power you give it. You keep that problem in place just as if it was stuck on a magnet.

When you have a strong interest in something, you tend to find it all around you. If you just bought a new red car, you'll see red cars all over the place. They were there before, but you didn't notice them because they weren't of interest to you.

It works for "negative" things too. If you are sure that most people are out to cheat you, then by golly, those are the kinds of people you will meet. Why? Because you have a strong focus on those kinds of people. They'll show up in your life because you believe in them. It's called the Law of Attraction.

But there is something you can do about it. Take a few minutes at the end of each day to go over what has gotten your attention the most, especially those things that have stirred up your feelings. For all the good things - bless them to increase them. But if you've been like a dog with a bone on some issue and you really don't want that situation to stay in your life, then put it in your mental trash can and let it go. If it is a long-standing problem, you might want to go to the front door, open it up, and kick that sucker out!

Life will bring to you what you are emotionally interested in. But the good news is that you get to make the choice of *what* that will be.

"Bestest"
Bread Pudding

My Favorite Dessert

houghout the years, cooks have always looked for ways to feed their families nutritious, delicious food at the least possible cost. In the era in which I grew up, "waste not, want not" was the byword. My parents and grandparents came through the "Great Depression," and that experience taught them to value everything and find a use for all they had.

Leftover food was not thrown away. It was saved and served again in a slightly different form for later meals. The fashion in my youth was to cut the crust off bread before sandwiches were made. The crusts weren't thrown away, however, but saved in a brown paper bag for later use. If somehow, a roll or slice of bread had dried out and wasn't good for regular eating, it was added to the bag. I would watch the bag fill up and anticipate the night its contents would be turned into the delightful dessert called "Bread Pudding." Despite its basic simplicity, there does seem to be some magic in making the "perfect" bread pudding, and it remains one of my favorite desserts to this day. If it's on the menu anywhere, I order it!

There are probably thousands of recipes for the dish, varying from region to region; and varying even more as members of individual families decided what particular combination of ingredients made it "bestest" for them.

My nationwide search for the best recipes turned up cooks from all over the country and bread pudding recipes that ranged from simple to complex, plus one with a "kick." Just reading these recipes makes me really hungry!

Aunt Anna's Apple Bread Pudding with Cinnamon Sauce

Wendy Nickel
Kiester, Minnesota

Ingredients:

Pudding

5 cups dry bread, cubed

1½ cups of cooking apples, peeled, cored and chopped

½ cup black walnuts

2½ cups cream

½ cup brown sugar, packed

1 teaspoon cinnamon

1½ teaspoons vanilla

½ teaspoon nutmeg

2 eggs, beaten

Sauce

1 cup brown sugar, packed

½ cup butter

1 cup cream

1 teaspoon cinnamon

½ teaspoon vanilla

Preparation:

Preheat oven to 350 degrees. In a greased two-quart casserole, place bread cubes, apples, and black walnuts. Mix together.

In a one-quart saucepan combine the cream with brown sugar and cinnamon. Heat until creamy, stirring constantly. Remove from heat and stir in vanilla.

Take a couple of tablespoons of cream mixture and add to beaten eggs to temper. Slowly add egg mixture to the saucepan, blend together and heat. Pour cream egg mixture over bread mixture. Bake at 350 degrees for 50 to 60 minutes.

Meanwhile, in a one-quart saucepan combine brown sugar, butter, and cream. Cook until smooth and creamy. Add cinnamon and vanilla. Cool. Serve over warm bread pudding.

Add extra calories with a dip of ice cream.

Behind the Recipe

Aunt Anna's Apple Bread Pudding
With Cinnamon Sauce

Aunt Anna was one of my mother's six sisters. She and Uncle Steve lived in Iowa for the majority of their lives. As a kid growing up I spend a lot of time with Aunt Anna and her family.

Each summer they would have a picnic out in the cow pasture. Anna and Steve loved to play games. If you didn't know the game they would teach you: dominos, buttons, cards, etc. With the games came a time for "visiting." We would always have lots of good food and good times (until the old men got to cheating at the games).

In the fall of the year when their apple trees were producing, Aunt Anna loved to make apple dumplings and share them with family and friends.

My husband, Don, loves bread pudding. When I created this recipe, putting apples in the bread pudding brought back fond memories of family and Aunt Anna's apple dumplings. Just wanted to have the best of both delicious desserts!

Wendy Nickel

Caribbean Buttermilk Bread PuddingWith Warm Caramel-Pecan Sauce

Janice Elder
Charlotte, North Carolina

Ingredients:

Pudding

1 16 ounce loaf Hawaiian bread,
¼ cup melted butter
5 eggs
2 large mangoes, peeled, seeded and diced
1 cup sugar
3 cups buttermilk
1 teaspoon vanilla extract
1 teaspoon ground cinnamon
¼ teaspoon ground nutmeg

Sauce

1 cup prepared caramel sauce
¾ cup chopped pecans, lightly toasted

Preparation:

Preheat oven to 350 degrees.

Spray a 2½ quart ovenproof baking dish with nonstick cooking spray.

Cut loaf of Hawaiian bread into 1 inch cubes and toast lightly.

In a large mixing bowl, toss the toasted bread cubes with the melted butter; reserve.

Lightly whisk the eggs until well blended; add mangoes, sugar, buttermilk, vanilla, cinnamon and nutmeg, blending well. Spoon mixture over the bread cubes, stirring gently. Blend well, then let sit for about 10 minutes.

Spoon mixture into prepared baking dish. Bake at 350 degrees for about an hour, or until the top is brown and the center still jiggles a little.

In a small saucepan over low heat, stir the caramel sauce and pecans together until heated through.

Serve the bread pudding either warm or chilled, with warm sauce spooned over.

Makes 6 to 8 servings.

Several years ago my husband and I enjoyed a romantic getaway to Jamaica. One dinner we especially remember was at a charming restaurant on the side of a cliff overlooking the ocean.

While I don't remember the main course, the wonderful bread pudding baked with mangoes and topped with a silky caramel sauce with pecans has remained indelibly imprinted in my memory. It took several experiments to come up with something close - the secrets are the tangy buttermilk and the Hawaiian bread.

It never fails to bring back island memories, no matter where it's served.

 Never ate anything as exotic as mangoes in bread pudding before, nor do I ever remember seeing "Aunt Bee" on TV use them. But never let it be said that the Mayberry Momma is not open to new ideas!

Dee Dee's Bread Pudding

Mary Lou Townsend
St. Augustine, Florida

Ingredients:

6 slices buttered toast, quartered
¼ cup raisins
¼ cup chopped nuts (pecans or walnuts)
2 eggs
¼ cup sugar
⅛ teaspoon salt
2 cups hot milk
1 teaspoon vanilla
4 teaspoons sugar
1 teaspoon cinnamon

Preparation:

Heat oven to 350 degrees. Grease casserole dish.

Layer buttered toast in 8 x 8 casserole dish, sprinkling raisins and nuts between layers of toast and on top. Combine eggs (slightly beaten) 1/4 sup sugar, salt, hot milk and vanilla. Pour over toast, raisins and nuts and let stand 10 minutes. Combine 4 teaspoons sugar and 1 teaspoon cinnamon and sprinkle on top. Bake for 30 minutes.

Grandma Pearl's Bread Pudding Sauce (This is the best part)

3 to 4 tablespoons butter
1 cup of sugar
1 egg, separated

Combine butter, sugar and egg yolk in top of double boiler. Simmer over boiling water, stirring occasionally, until sugar dissolves. Beat egg white until just stiff and fold into sauce.

Serve pudding warm or cold, with generous topping of Sauce.

Serves 6-8

Every one in the family loved bread pudding, and it was a great way to use up stale bread. My sister-in-law, Dee Dee, experimented until she declared this to be the best recipe for bread pudding. But what really makes the bread pudding delicious is the sugar sauce always made by our grandmother, Pearl. You just can't have one without the other!

Upon marrying my southern husband over fifty years ago, this is one of the first things I learned how to cook from his family.

It sounds Dee Dee Licious!

PaPa's Favorite Custard Bread Pudding With Whiskey Sauce

Denise Marcelle Boudreaux Wilkes
St. Augustine, Florida

Ingredients:

Pudding

1 dozen large eggs, room temperature, separated (save whites for meringue next day)
1 loaf of long French style Bread - stale
2 cups sugar
4 cans evaporated milk
¼ pound butter (1 stick - cut into pats)
1 tablespoon pure vanilla extract
1 tablespoon cinnamon
2 cups large golden raisins (previously soaked in bourbon or whiskey overnight or longer and kept in refrigerator)

Meringue

Whites from 12 eggs
2 teaspoons cream of tartar
¾ cup of sugar

Sauce

¼ cup cornstarch
½ cup cold water
3 cups Half and Half (not fat free)
⅓ to ½ cup high quality whiskey or bourbon
1 tablespoon nutmeg (freshly ground)

Preparation:

Mix the egg yolks and sugar until light colored. Add evaporated milk and vanilla and beat well.

Break up the loaf of French Bread into small chunks and put in a large buttered roasting type pan. Sprinkle in the raisins. Pour the egg mixture into the pan being sure to get all the bread well saturated. Sprinkle cinnamon all over and cover with butter pats. Cover tightly with plastic wrap and refrigerate 24 hours. (Overnight at the least)

When ready to bake, remove cover and place in a preheated 325 degree oven for 1½ hours. Top will be medium browned. Test by a knife in the center to be sure it's done.

To make the Meringue, about 15 minutes before pudding is to be done beat egg whites with cream of tartar until foamy. Add 1/4 cup sugar, beat some more - add 1/4 cup more sugar, beat again - add last 1/4 cup sugar and beat until stiff.

When bread pudding is done, take it out of the oven and load the meringue all over the top, being sure to seal it to the edges. (I use a metal spatula moistened with water.) Place it back in the oven. Leave the oven door slightly open and turn on the boiler. DO NOT WALK AWAY. At the first signs of golden brown peaks on the meringue, remove the pudding from the oven and turn off the oven.

To make the whiskey or bourbon sauce, blend cornstarch with cold water in a small bowl. Pour the Half and Half into a saucepan and warm over low heat to simmering. Whisk in the cornstarch water and continue to simmer until it's as thick as you like. Turn off the heat, remove from burner and slowly whisk in 1/3 to 1/2 cup of high quality whiskey or bourbon.

Dust the meringue with nutmeg. Serve the bread pudding while still warm. Put the sauce in a serving bowl with a ladle for pouring over the servings of pudding.

This delicious bread pudding can be enjoyed cold as well, if there any leftovers!

Makes 24 Servings

My mom always made bread pudding because in New Orleans we had French Bread every day with supper. By the end of the week there would be enough left over to make the pudding. The staler the bread was, the better, because it was very light and easy to break. No bread anywhere else is as good as in New Orleans, but you need a light bread, and French Bread works best.

We were a large family—six kids—so my mom didn't go in for "fancy." I have modified the way she made it. Because my dad and I love egg custard, or flan as it is also called, I have added a lot more eggs to make for a very rich dessert.

Many whiskey sauces call for sugar, but I think it should be more whiskey flavored and less sweet so you will savor the flavor. I prefer bourbon.

My favorite bourbon is Woodford Reserve and my choice is Earthbound Organic Farms for the raisins and Pet for the evaporated milk. I like the way Pet milk tastes, probably because that was what my Aunt Marie always used to make her incredibly delicious fudge. She has passed away and I am carrying on her tradition. Mine's very good, but hers was "perfect."

When I was a little girl my job was to break the pecans - you never chop them with a knife - blend the sugar and cocoa, butter the platters and clean up when it was finished. But that's another recipe for another time.

Maybe one of these years I'll tell you about my awesome pralines. I sure loved to eat pralines when we went to the French Quarter! I have been making them for about 20 years and my friends tell me they are fabulous. Actually, they are!

Denise Marcelle Boudreaux Wilkes

Lawsie Mercy, I think I gained a couple of pounds just reading the recipe! For you folks in teetotaling households, just substitute your favorite non-alcoholic flavored liquid -- you may have to change the amount somewhat. I love the Southern Praline Mix put out by the folks at the Savannah Cinnamon Company. Have heard that rum or amaretto flavored concoctions work well also.

If they were serving this where I was eatin' a meal, I would definitely have to eat dessert first!

Another Helping of Soul Food

Stop "Bad-Mouthing" Yourself!

*D*own South we've got a phrase that describes criticizing and complaining about someone. We'll call it "bad-mouthing" that person.

Truth is, the person you are most likely to bad-mouth is *yourself*! You wouldn't dare talk about your friends the way you speak about yourself.

"I'm such a klutz."

"I'll never learn how to do this."

"No point in even trying, I know I'll mess it up."

Did you know that every time you say or think negative things about yourself, you actually make yourself weaker? Scientists have discovered that the body responds to mental images and feelings and strengthens or weakens as a result. A sprinter would never make it across the finish line in first place if he was telling himself " There's no way I can win this race."

Get yourself an invisible "Cancel" stamp and use it every time you catch yourself being negative about yourself and your talents and abilities. Use that sucker frequently. Then see things turn around and watch yourself soar!

Casseroles That Cook!

Food to Share
and Plenty to Spare

*M*illions of church "pot luck" dinners each year depend on the delicious and creative casserole dishes served up by the parishioners. Their variety is virtually endless.

The long tables in the basement of Central Methodist Church in Mount Airy, North Carolina fairly groaned under the weight of so many scrumptious offerings. All us young'ns would check out each one as they were brought in, trying to obey our elder's admonitions to keep our fingers out of them. Whispers flew quickly between us.

"The stuff in the green bowl—Sally's mother made that. It's bound to be good."

"You don't want what's in that brown bowl. Old Mizz Johnson brought that." Bobby said, his face scrunched up in disgust, remembering what her previous offerings had tasted like.

As I got older, I realized that Mrs. Johnson's casserole was probably quite good. It was just healthier fare than we kids wanted in those childhood years.

Actually, "casserole" is the type of container that the ingredients are baked in. That accounts for the fact that a casserole dish may contain ingredients that are appropriate for every kind of meal - breakfast, lunch, dinner, and everything in between - and after. Yes, there are dessert casseroles, and mighty fine ones indeed!

Cindy's "Git Along Home" Chicken Casserole

Cindy Meadows
Ft. Walton Beach, Florida

Ingredients:

1 (3-4 pound) broiler-fryer

1 large onion

2 stalks celery, chopped

3 tablespoons butter or margarine

1 28 ounce can tomatoes, drained and chopped

4 drops hot sauce

Salt to taste

8 ounces uncooked vermicelli or spaghetti

½ green pepper, coarsely chopped

2 cloves garlic, minced

1 can cream of mushroom soup

1 tablespoon Worcestershire sauce

⅛ teaspoon pepper

1 cup shredded medium cheddar cheese

Preparation:

Place chicken in a large pot or Dutch oven, cover with salted water. Bring to a boil; cover, reduce heat and simmer 1 hour or until tender. Remove chicken, let cool. Bone chicken, and cut meat into bite-sized pieces. Set aside.

Preheat oven to 350 degrees

Reserve ¼ cup chicken broth; set aside. Bring remaining broth to a boil. Break vermicelli or spaghetti in half and cook in broth 10-12 minutes or until tender: drain well. Return spaghetti or vermicelli to Dutch oven; set aside.

Sauté onion, green pepper, celery and garlic in butter until tender; add to spaghetti.

Combine cream of mushroom soup, and ¼ cup reserved broth and stir into spaghetti mixture

Add tomatoes and chicken; stir well. Add seasonings, mixing well.

Spoon the mixture into lightly greased 13x9x2 inch baking dish. Sprinkle with shredded cheese. Bake at 350 degrees for 15 to 20 minutes or until cheese melts.

Serves 8-10

All the fans of The Andy Griffith Show will remember how many times Sheriff Andy Taylor, Opie and The Darlings sang the old folk song, "Cindy" with its chorus of "Git along home, Cindy, Cindy, git along home."

Although our winning cook wasn't aware of it, Andy Griffith's wife is named Cindy also.

If you "don't have all day," as the old saying goes, Momma suggests you pick up a cooked chicken at the store, along with canned chicken broth for a "short cut" version of this great recipe. Can't guarantee it will be as tasty as Cindy's though.

Behind the Recipe

Cindy's "Git Along Home" Chicken Casserole

When all the family members were out of town one time, I decided to see if I could come up with a good, filling dish. Something that would fit the definition of a "nice home-cooked meal."

This recipe was the result. Once I made it for the family it was a big hit. After my sister, Pat, got the recipe from me, she has cooked it for every family event and all those potluck dinners at church.

Although the ingredients are simple, the dish is full of flavor. You can refrigerate the leftovers (if there are any) as they are great reheated, even in the microwave. In fact, the leftovers from this dish are out-of-the-world delicious.

I can't wait for my sweet husband, Hap, to finish his deployment with the Air Force in Iraq.

Surely my scrumptious Chicken Casserole will be something for him to "Git Along Home" for!

Cindy Meadows

Getting to Know the Grand Prize Winner– Cindy Meadows

As Cindy explained it, "I was piled up in bed watching a rerun of *The Andy Griffith Show*," when she received the call telling her that she had won the Grand Prize in the Mayberry Momma's™ national recipe contest. Cindy, a big fan of the show said that when she read in her local newspaper about the contest, it was the "Mayberry" factor that caused her to enter.

"I've always called my hometown of Ft. Walton Beach 'Mayberry' so I'm doubly excited about winning." Cindy's great-grandfather, John Thomas Brooks, was the founder of Ft. Walton Beach and she's lived there all her life. All of her family still live in the area and are very active in the community.

Cindy told us she enjoys snow skiing, water skiing, roller skating, horse back riding, gardening, and bowling. She is very proud of Hap's 10 year old son, Logan, and said, "One day he'll be a professional baseball player. You can count on that." On the other side of the generations, Cindy very much values time spent with her grandmother, Mema. "She is such a delight, and 95 years young!"

It's almost surprising that Cindy was trying to "think up" a new recipe. Certainly there are a lot of good ones in the 500 cookbooks she has collected! But Cindy really enjoys cooking, as well as the challenge of coming up with new dishes.

Cindy's husband, Master Sergeant Happy (Hap) Ray Meadows, is stationed at Eglin Field in the 728th Air Control Squadron, the "Demons." Cindy entered the Squadron's annual chili and cornbread contest. She won the contest with her "Hap Hazards Hell's Half Acre Chili." Her unnamed cornbread recipe, also with chili as an ingredient, took that category also.

Time and again Cindy returned to talking about how wonderful her husband, Hap, is and how much she misses him. Master Sergeant Meadows plans to retire from the Air Force next year after 26 years in service. Cindy eagerly awaits his return from Iraq, which is scheduled just in time for the two of them to enjoy the contest's Grand Prize—a cruise to the Caribbean!

Trailer Park Casserole

Patricia Padgett
Cathedral City, California

Ingredients:

1 package flat egg noodles

3 to 4 chicken breasts

1 package 4-cheese or Mexican blend grated cheese

1 (10¾ oz) can cream of mushroom soup

1 (10¾ oz) can cream of celery soup

1 (8 oz) carton light sour cream

½ (16 oz) package of Ritz crackers or similar brand

1 sweet onion, chopped finely

¼ cup melted butter or margarine

Salt & pepper to taste

Preparation:

Preheat oven to 350 degrees

Put chicken breasts in cooking pan, cover with water and bring to a boil. Reduce heat to simmer and cook thoroughly. Cool, slice into small pieces.

Cook noodles in accordance with package directions until done; drain, set aside. Lightly grease large casserole pan with cooking spray. Crush all crackers and layer half in bottom of dish.

Combine chicken pieces, chopped onion, soups, sour cream and salt and pepper. Layer half of the chicken mixture on top of crackers.

Add layer of noodles. Add a layer of grated cheese. Top with remaining half of chicken mixture.

Finish with remaining crackers and drizzle with melted butter.

Bake for 25 minutes.

Serves 10 Keeps well for leftovers and heats well in microwave

My son created this recipe for a group function. He was an experienced cook, but had no casserole recipe appropriate for the occasion. A check of the cupboard and refrigerator revealed the above ingredients and an idea was born. Glad to say that the results were very well received.

Commenting on his creation, he lamented that it was not really "gourmet"—in fact, was more "trailer park," with its humble ingredients. We have since enjoyed it many times and still refer to it as his "Trailer Park Casserole."

"Mexican Macaroni" Stovetop Casserole

Mary Bilyeu
Ann Arbor, Michigan

Ingredients:

1½ pound ground beef

½ red onion, chopped

4 garlic cloves, minced

2 cups dry macaroni

2 cups fire-roasted crushed tomatoes

2 cups water

1 teaspoon salt

½ teaspoon pepper

4 teaspoons taco seasoning mix

8 ounces extra-sharp cheddar cheese, grated

Preparation:

In a large, deep-sided skillet, brown ground beef over medium-high heat; drain. Add onion and garlic, and sauté just until onion is translucent.

Add macaroni, tomatoes, water, salt, pepper and taco seasoning; stir to combine. (I prefer Muir Glen Organic Fire Roasted Tomatoes and Old El Paso Taco Seasoning.) Cover and bring to a boil; then lower heat to medium and cook 30 minutes. Uncover, then stir in grated cheese. Serve hot to hungry family and friends! Is great with a tossed salad and good bread.

Serves 4-6

This is the kind of comforting food that would be served in Mayberry. Meals like this welcome a family to the dinner table after a long day. It can easily be taken to a church supper, or can be made quickly to provide solace to friends and neighbors in times of trouble.

I created it one cold February night when a good hot meal was in order, but there was no time to run to the store for special items.

Appreciating family and good wholesome food—the simple pleasures in life—isn't that what Mayberry is all about?

Pauline's Crockpot Lasagna

Wendy Nickel
Keister, Minnesota

Ingredients:

1 pound ground turkey, browned

1 medium onion, chopped

2 cloves garlic, minced

1 teaspoon salt

12 ounces mini-lasagna prepared according to package directions

1 (28 ounce) jar spaghetti sauce

1½ cups large curd style cottage cheese

1 (8 ounce) bag mozzarella cheese, shredded

Preparations:

Mix all ingredients (except cheese) together in a 4-quart crockpot. Cook on high for 2 hours, or it can cook longer at low heat.

Add cheese 30 minutes before serving.

Pauline Nickel is my mother-in-law who is one excellent cook. No matter when people stop in she can serve a tasty meal. She is my inspiration for this easy recipe. We love to share ideas and recipes.

The son of a family friend once said to my husband, "Don, you are really lucky because you have a wife and a mom who both can cook." *A very nice compliment to us both.*

This recipe is great for when you don't have time to prepare a meal after work. Team this up with a fresh spinach salad and garlic toast and you've got a hearty supper.

When I was raising three children, while trying to make a living in the marketplace, I couldn't have done it without the Crock-Pot! Early in the morning I'd place all the ingredients for a good stew in the pot, turn it on low and leave it to do its thing. Before my teenage daughter left for her job at a fast food restaurant in the afternoon, she'd help herself to a bowl of stew. Her brother would grab a fast bite before he headed out to "bum around" with his friends. Then my youngest son would come in from Little League practice "starving" and head straight for the Crock-Pot. I was the last one in, and really appreciative of not having to cook a meal.

Oh, and I do want to thank the "Hamburger Helper" folks. They got me through many a crisis. Couldn't count how many helpings of "Cheeseburger Macaroni" were consumed.

There are just times in life that a Simple Supper is Super!

Aunt Bee's Chicken And Rice

Janine L. Johnson
Orlando, Florida

Ingredients:

2-3 lb. fryer chicken, cut up
1 can of cream of chicken sup
1 can of cream of mushroom soup
2 soup cans of water
1½ cups uncooked rice
Salt and pepper to taste
Dried parsley and paprika to sprinkle

Preparation:

Preheat oven to 350 degrees

Set aside 2 tablespoons of each of the soups and stir together in a small bowl.

In 13 x 9 baking dish, spoon the remaining soup and slowly stir in the water and rice. Place chicken pieces on top of rice mixture. Spoon reserved soup mixture on top of chicken pieces.

Sprinkle with dried parsley, salt and pepper to taste and paprika for color. Cover and bake for 1 hour. Uncover and bake another 15-30 minutes until all water is absorbed by the rice and chicken is lightly browned.

Makes 4-6 servings

This recipe originated with my mother many years ago and has been revised somewhat to suit my tastes. It is so simple and easy, but delicious and nice enough for company. It can be made with any chicken pieces.

If you're really in a hurry, it can even be fixed with precooked rice and canned chicken; just omit the water and heat in the oven enough to blend the flavors and lightly brown the top of the casserole.

My Internet moniker is "Aunt Bee of Orlando," so I now call it Aunt Bee's recipe!

SECTION THIRTEEN

Soul Food for Your Journey

Make God Your First Thought —Not Your Last Resort

Drawing on strength from our spiritual beliefs should be the bedrock of our lives—not something we only turn to in times of trouble.

How many times have we been in a religious service and repeated "God is the source of my life. In Him I live and move and have my being." But when a challenge comes, don't we often flail around looking desperately for a way out? Then, when our rational minds can't find a solution, when nothing else seems to be working, we "beg" God to help us!

If you really believe that God is the source of your life, all of your problems are just in the world of appearances—not the world of Spiritual Truth. When you really know that, your first thought is to reaffirm your connection to the Divine. Divine Wisdom, Divine Power, Divine Peace. All of those are available to you immediately and consistently! It sounds simple, but it ain't always easy, is it?

There was a time when other people seemed to have the power to make my life miserable and threaten my well-being in every area. But after many weeks of fear and mental anguish, I remembered the words of the 23rd Psalm, "Yea though I walk through the valley of the shadow of death, I will fear no evil."

Life can be hard work sometimes, can't it? Well, it took time and lots of consistent spiritual work on my part, but after a while I started to respond differently. Every time I began to feel nervous or afraid I would just say to myself "God is the only power in my life! Everything else is just an appearance. It's not real. I believe in a different truth."

I would repeat it over and over again, day after day. A few weeks later I received a letter that completely changed the situation and removed all of the previous threats.

You need to stay connected to the Spirit on a daily basis. Then, when trouble rears its ugly head, all you have to do is strongly reaffirm that connection.

With God as your first thought, you'll never need a last resort.

Epilogue

Momma Gets
the Last Word

*W*hen my first book, *Memories of Mayberry*, was published, the first thing everybody asked me was, "Why didn't you put some recipes in the book?"

Over the months I heard that question many times, and I finally had to agree; a book about Southern roots just calls out for food!

So, I embarked on a nationwide search to find some "down-home" recipes that would be "soul satisfying." We received some fabulous offerings from all points of the compass in this great country. I'm sorry that we couldn't include them all.

These days I live in St. Augustine, Florida, but I always say that at any given time half of North Carolina is in Florida and vice versa. You may have noticed that several recipes from St. Augustine are included in the book, and you may have wondered about that.

Two things happened; the local media really played up the contest and a lot of folks from the area entered. Also, as the oldest city in North America,

St. Augustine is a magnet for people (so many of them visit and decide they want to come back,) so a lot of really creative cooks from all over the country end up living here!

However, when the recipes went to the chefs for judging, they had no names or places or stories with them - just the bare recipes. The judges had no idea where any recipe was from. In the end, a number of recipes from good cooks that had settled in St. Augustine stood out. Didn't think it was fittin' to penalize them for that.

What was most "soul satisfying" for me was getting to know the fine folks whose recipes are included in this book. They represent a broad spectrum of this great country. I personally called all those whose recipes were chosen for inclusion. All were people I feel privileged to have had an opportunity to interact with.

Some were world travelers and brought influences from other places into their recipes. Others were more rooted to their home bases, revising dishes that had been handed down from generation to generation.

Many of them had difficulty writing down all of the elements of preparing the dish, since they were just doin' what they remembered their mother or grandmother did. All of them were women who really enjoyed cooking and serving good food. They connected with the idea of food, family and fellowship.

That's the "Mayberry" spirit! And I'm delighted to celebrate it with them and with you!

Jewell Mitchell Kutzer
aka the Mayberry Momma™